D1236716

Leaf-Cutting Ants

by Helen Frost

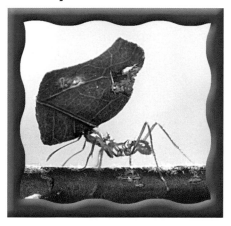

Consulting Editor: Gail Saunders-Smith, Ph.D.

Consultants: James K. Wetterer, Associate Professor, Biology and Environmental Studies, Honors College, Florida Atlantic University

Pebble Books

an imprint of Capstone Press
Mankato, Minnesota

Pebble Books are published by Capstone Press
151 Good Counsel Drive, P.O. Box 669, Mankato, Minnesota 56002
http://www.capstone-press.com

1 2 3 4 5 6 07 06 05 04 03 02

Library of Congress Cataloging-in-Publication Data
Frost, Helen, 1949–
     Leaf-cutting ants / by Helen Frost.
     p. cm.—(Rain forest animals)
     Summary: Simple text and photographs present the features and behavior of an
unusual species of ants.
     Includes bibliographical references (p. 23) and index.
     ISBN 0-7368-1457-4 (hardcover)
     1. Leaf-cutting ants—Juvenile literature. [1. Leaf-cutting ants. 2. Ants. 3. Rain
forest animals.] I. Title.
QL568.F7 F75 2003
595.79'6—dc21   2002001230

Note to Parents and Teachers

The Rain Forest Animals series supports national science standards
related to life science. This book describes and illustrates leaf-cutting
ants that live in tropical rain forests. The photographs support
early readers in understanding the text. The repetition of words
and phrases helps early readers learn new words. This book also
introduces early readers to subject-specific vocabulary words, which
are defined in the Words to Know section. Early readers may need
assistance to read some words and to use the Table of Contents,
Words to Know, Read More, Internet Sites, and Index/Word List
sections of the book.

Table of Contents

Leaf-cutting ants
are insects.

jaws

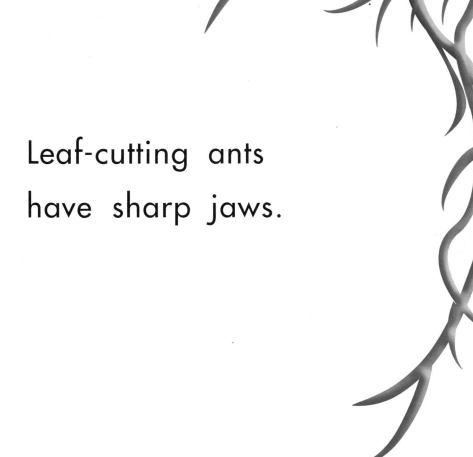

Leaf-cutting ants
have sharp jaws.

places where some leaf-cutting ants live

8

Some leaf-cutting ants live in tropical rain forests in Central and South America.

emergent layer

canopy layer

understory layer

forest floor

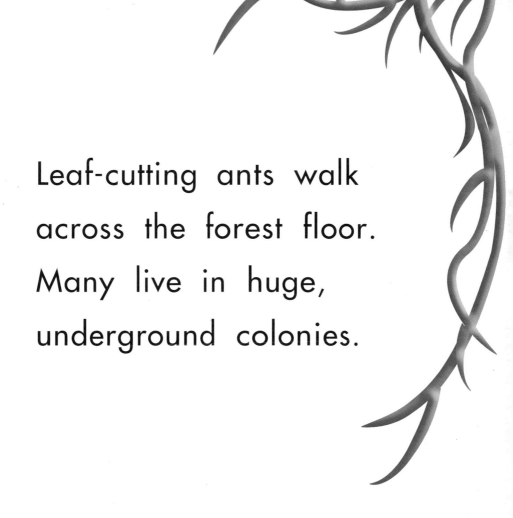

Leaf-cutting ants walk across the forest floor. Many live in huge, underground colonies.

Some leaf-cutting ants climb trees to find leaves. They cut pieces of leaves with their jaws.

Some leaf-cutting ants
cut leaves at night.

Leaf-cutting ants
carry the leaves
to their colony.

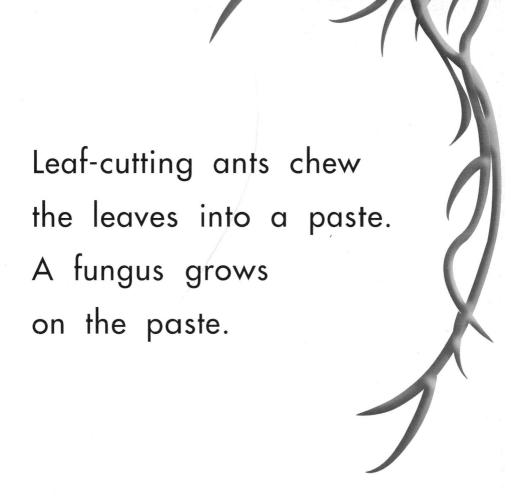

Leaf-cutting ants chew
the leaves into a paste.
A fungus grows
on the paste.

Leaf-cutting ants
eat the fungus.

Words to Know

colony—a large group of insects that live together; leaf-cutting ant colonies can have more than one million ants.

forest floor—the bottom layer of the rain forest; almost no sunlight reaches the forest floor.

fungus—a type of living thing that has no leaves, flowers, or roots; leaf-cutting ants eat a kind of fungus.

insect—a small animal with six legs, three main body sections, and a hard outer shell

jaw—a mouthpart used to grab, bite, and chew; leaf-cutting ants have sharp jaws.

paste—a soft, wet mixture

tropical rain forest—a thick area of trees in a warm place where rain falls almost every day

underground—below the ground; leaf-cutting ants build colonies in underground chambers connected by tunnels.

Read More

Fowler, Allan. *Inside an Ant Colony.* Rookie Read-About Science. Danbury, Conn.: Children's Press, 1998.

Steele, Christy. *Ants.* Animals of the Rain Forest. Austin, Texas: Steadwell Books, 2001.

Stefoff, Rebecca. *Ant.* Living Things. New York: Benchmark Books, 1998.

Venn, Cecilia. *Ants and Other Social Insects.* Animals of the World. Chicago: World Book, 2000.

Internet Sites

Fungus-Growing Ants
http://www.antcolony.org/leafcutter/leafcuttermain.htm

Insecta Inspecta World: Leafcutting Ants
http://www.insecta-inspecta.com/ants/leafcutter

Leaf-Cutter Ants
http://www.phoenixzoo.org/pages/animals/leaf_cutter.html

Index/Word List

Word Count: 85
Early-Intervention Level: 10

Editorial Credits

Martha E. H. Rustad, editor; Linda Clavel and Heidi Meyer, cover designers; Jennifer Schonborn, interior illustrator; Angi Gahler, book designer; Wanda Winch, photo researcher; Karen Risch, product planning editor

Photo Credits

Digital Vision, 8
Jay Ireland and Georgienne E. Bradley, 12
Minden Pictures/Mark Moffett, cover, 4, 6, 14, 18, 20
Thomas C. Boyden, 16
USDA/ARS/Scott Bauer, 1

The author thanks the children's section staff at the Allen County Public Library in Fort Wayne, Indiana, for research assistance.